Paperback ISBN: 978-1-63731-995-6   Hardcover ISBN: 978-1-63731-996-3

Copyright © SEL Enterprise
Printed 2024 - All rights Reserved

We reserve all rights to copyright, illustrations, and design.

She loved to gaze at holiday plans,
To see what fun they'd bring,
But one brisk morning, to her **SURPRISE**,
Some important dates were missing!

She called upon her friend, Frosty,
"Hey, did you catch a clue?
My holidays are **DISAPPEARING**—
What am I gonna do?"

December frowned and thought a bit,
"That wind was **STRONG**, it's true,
But wind can't take away my dates—
Something else is askew."

She wandered to the reindeer barn,
Where Prancer stood so tall,
"Do you know **WHERE** my dates have gone?
This puzzle's got me stalled!"

Prancer chuckled, "Well, I've heard,
'Bout a Hopper who flies by,
He skips through time like it's a game,
And **ZOOMS** right through the sky."

Aha!" December snapped her fingers,
"The Holiday Hopper's near!
He's leaping through my **FAVORITE** days,
But now I'm in the clear!"

She set a trap with holiday **CHEER**,
And marked each date with care,
With candy canes and shining lights,
She knew she'd catch him there.

She hid behind the snowy drifts,
And waited, still as night,
The air was crisp, the stars were **BRIGHT**,
Her heart felt warm and light.

Then **SUDDENLY**, the Hopper zoomed,
He laughed from here to there.
He reached to snag another day,
But got caught in her snare!

"**GOTCHA!**" December laughed happily,
"No more skipping days for you!
Let's savor each and every holiday,
Having fun and being grateful too!"

Now December's days are full of joy,
Her friends all gather near,
They share the **WARMTH** of winter nights,
And spread their holiday cheer!

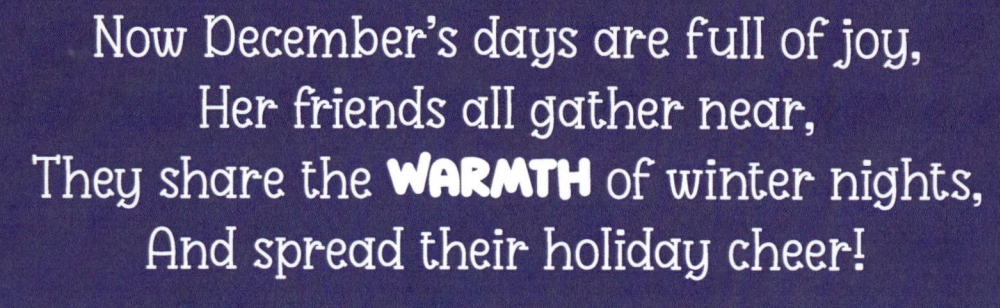

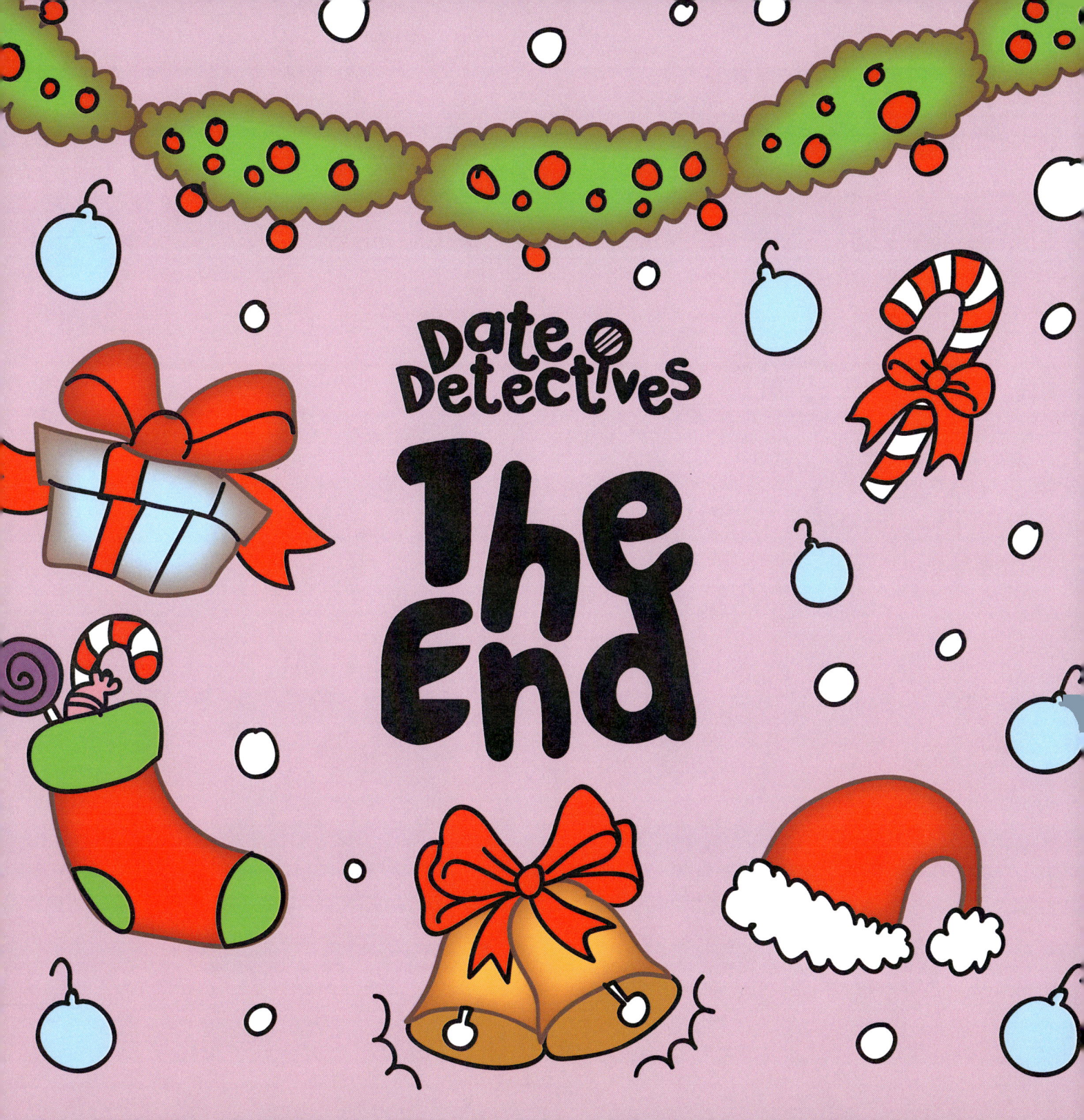

CRAFT ACTIVITY: SNOWY ORNAMENTS

YOU'LL NEED:
* WHITE OR LIGHT-COLORED PAPER (OR COFFEE FILTERS)
* SCISSORS
* STRING OR RIBBON
* MARKERS, CRAYONS, OR GLITTER (OPTIONAL FOR DECORATION)
* HOLE PUNCH (OPTIONAL)

INSTRUCTIONS:

1. FOLD YOUR PAPER:
Start with a square piece of paper. If you're using regular printer paper, cut it into a square by folding one corner diagonally and cutting off the excess rectangle.

- Fold the square in half to form a triangle.
- Fold the triangle in half again to make a smaller triangle.
- Fold it one more time so it becomes an even smaller triangle.

2. CUT YOUR SNOWFLAKE:
- Now, grab your scissors! Along the edges of your folded triangle, cut out small shapes like triangles, circles, or half-moons. These will create the intricate pattern of your snowflake. Be creative with your cuts, but don't cut all the way through the folded edges—leave some space to hold the snowflake together.
- Tip: The more cuts you make, the more detailed your snowflake will be!

3. UNFOLD YOUR SNOWFLAKE:
- Carefully unfold your paper to reveal your beautiful, one-of-a-kind snowflake. You should see a symmetrical pattern emerge.

4. ADD DECORATIVE ELEMENTS (OPTIONAL):
- If you want to add some extra sparkle or color, now's the time! You can decorate your snowflake with markers, crayons, or add glitter along the edges for a festive touch.

5. PUNCH A HOLE FOR HANGING:
- Use a hole punch at the top of your snowflake (or carefully make a small hole with your scissors), then loop a piece of string or ribbon through it.

6. HANG YOUR SNOWFLAKE:
- Find the perfect spot on your Christmas tree, window, or anywhere in your home to hang your snowy ornament. It's sure to add a touch of winter cheer!

www.ingramcontent.com/pod-product-compliance
Lightning Source LLC
Chambersburg PA
CBRC091454160426
43209CB00024B/1889